Little Scientists®

A "hands-on" approach to learning

Fun With
Mixing and Chemistry

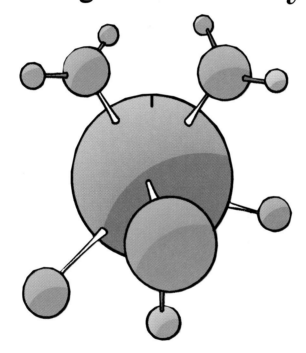

Dear Parents,

Young children are natural scientists, curious about the world around them. They have an infinite capacity to learn and are eager to know why and how things work the way they do. *Little Scientists, Hands-On Activities* begins with the simple questions most children ask and then shows them how to explore and find out for themselves. Our acclaimed Little Scientists, "hands-on" approach instills in children a passion for the exciting world of science and helps children develop specific scientific skills that will provide a strong foundation for later learning.

With this book, you can join me on a journey into the wonders of "Mixing and Chemistry." Together we will discover the unlocked secrets of chemicals and learn how to create bouncing balls, homemade ice cream, really sticky glue, and many other exciting things.

Your Little Scientist can email me at
Dr_Heidi@Little-Scientists.com

Wishing you success,

Dr. Heidi

Little Scientists®

A "hands-on" approach to learning

Fun With
Mixing and Chemistry

Heidi Gold-Dworkin, Ph.D.

McGraw-Hill

New York   San Francisco   Washington, D.C.
Auckland   Bogotá   Caracas   Lisbon   London   Madrid   Mexico City
Milan   Montreal   New Delhi   San Juan   Singapore   Sydney   Tokyo   Toronto

*This book is dedicated to my children
Aviva, Olivia, and Robert*

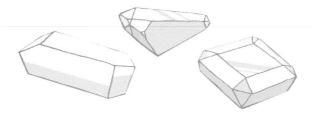

This book would not have been possible
without the contributions from the following
staff members at Little Scientists:®
Ronda Margolis
Avi Ornstein
Linda Burian
Bec Luty

I would like to thank my devoted family especially:
my husband, Jay; mom, Jacqueline, and sister, Stacey.

McGraw-Hill

*A Division of The **McGraw-Hill** Companies*

Copyright © 2000 by **The McGraw-Hill Companies, Inc**. All rights reserved. Printed in the United States of America. Except as permitted under the United States Copyright Act of 1976, no part of this publication may be reproduced or distributed in any form or by any means, or stored in a data base or retrieval system, without the prior written permission of the publisher or the author.

pbk   3 4 5 6 7 8 9 0 QPD / QPD   0 9 8 7 6 5 4 3 2 1

ISBN 0-07-134825-5

Library of Congress Cataloging-in-Publication data applied for.

McGraw-Hill books are available at special quantity discounts to use as premiums and sales promotions. For more information, please write to the Director of Special Sales, McGraw-Hill, Two Penn Plaza, New York, NY 10021. Or contact your local bookstore.

Acquisitions editor: Mary Loebig Giles
Senior editing supervisor: Patricia V. Amoroso
Senior production supervisors: Clare B. Stanley and Charles Annis
Left page illustrations: Robert K. Ullman <r.k.ullman@worldnet.att.net>
Right page illustrations: K. Almadingen <dzbersin@aol.com>
Book design: Jaclyn J. Boone <bookdesign@rcn.com>

Printed and bound by Quebecor/Dubuque.

Contents

Hi. I am Dr. Heidi.
Let's follow my Little Scientists® friend, Olivia, as she discovers the exciting world of chemistry. Together, we will explore how to make bouncing balls, homemade ice cream, and really sticky glue.

What are chemicals?

Chemicals are in everything — the air we breathe, the food we eat, and the clothes we wear. Even our bodies are made of chemicals! Let's see how many chemicals you can find in your house.

You will *need*
- Toothpaste
- Can of soup
- Glass cleaner
- Package of frozen dinner
- Shampoo

1. Look at the ingredient lists on different packages and bottles for the names of chemicals.

2. Write the names on a piece of paper as a list in alphabetical order.

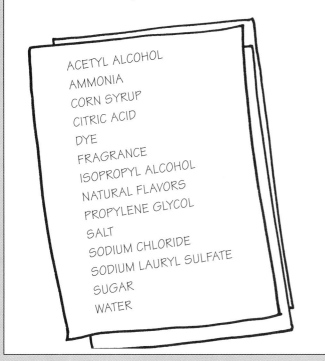

ACETYL ALCOHOL
AMMONIA
CORN SYRUP
CITRIC ACID
DYE
FRAGRANCE
ISOPROPYL ALCOHOL
NATURAL FLAVORS
PROPYLENE GLYCOL
SALT
SODIUM CHLORIDE
SODIUM LAURYL SULFATE
SUGAR
WATER

3. Star the ones that are found in more than one package.

ACETYL ALCOHOL
AMMONIA
CORN SYRUP *
CITRIC ACID *
DYE *
FRAGRANCE
ISOPROPYL ALCOHOL
NATURAL FLAVORS *
PROPYLENE GLYCOL *
SALT *
SODIUM CHLORIDE *
SODIUM LAURYL SULFATE
SUGAR
WATER *

3

How small are the chemicals in these boxes and bottles?

4

All **chemicals** consist of **molecules** that are made up of even smaller **atoms**. They are far too small for us to see, even with the most powerful microscopes!

You will need
- Sheet of paper
- 1 cracker
- Water
- Toothpick

1. Tear the sheet of paper into small pieces.

2. Take one piece and tear it into smaller pieces.

3. Keep doing this until the pieces are as small as you can make them. The smallest piece still contains billions and billions of atoms! Atoms are so tiny that no one has ever seen one with the naked eye.

4. Repeat this with a cracker on the surface of a table. Make the pieces as small as you are able.

5. Now try this with a drop of water on the table. Use a toothpick to separate the drop into smaller and smaller droplets.

The smallest droplet of water still contains billions and billions of water molecules! No one has ever seen a single molecule of water. If one drop of water was divided between all of the people in this country, we would each have more than ten trillion molecules of water!

If atoms and molecules are too small to see, how do scientists know what they are like?

One way scientists are able to learn the shape of molecules
is by studying their crystals.

1. Place some table salt in one cup. Add a little water to the cup and stir with a spoon.

You will need
- Table salt
- 2 clear cups
- Water
- 2 spoons
- 2 cotton swabs
- 2 sheets of black construction paper
- Epsom salt (from a pharmacy)

2. If all of the salt disappears, add some more and stir again. Continue doing this until you can see some salt in the bottom of the cup. This is called a *saturated solution*.

3. Dip the cotton swab into the saturated solution of table salt and use it to write TABLE SALT on one sheet of black paper.

4. Repeat steps 1 – 3, except use Epsom salt instead of table salt.

5. When the water evaporates, study the shapes of the crystals, which are the remains of the salt solutions that are visible on the black paper.

Crystals are a visible form of molecules that make it
much easier for scientists to see and study their shapes.

What do molecules look like?

Make your own models to find out what some molecules look like. Select different colored gumdrops to stand for different types of atoms. (Each gumdrop will represent a single atom.) Use toothpicks to connect the gumdrops. Try to match the pictures shown below.

You will need
- 21 gumdrops of 4 different colors
- Box of toothpicks

hydrogen gas
H_2

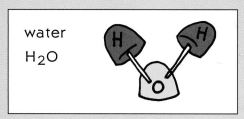

water
H_2O

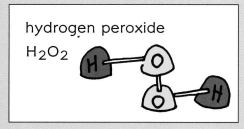

hydrogen peroxide
H_2O_2

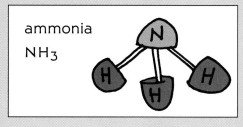

ammonia
NH_3

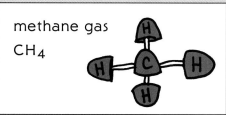

methane gas
CH_4

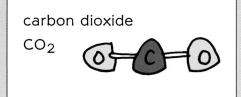

carbon dioxide
CO_2

1. Select one colored gumdrop for each of the following elements:

carbon C

hydrogen H

nitrogen N

oxygen O

2. Using toothpicks and the correct colored gumdrops, make models of the molecules listed in the boxes to the left.

For example, if a red gumdrop represents a hydrogen atom, take two red gumdrops and connect them with one toothpick to make a model of a molecule of hydrogen gas.

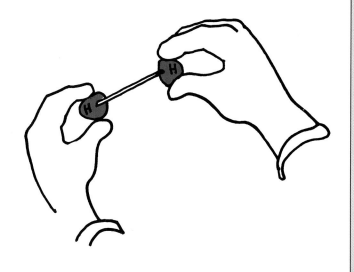

What does
a big molecule
look like?

Let's try to make a model of a larger molecule — fruit sugar.

You will *need*
• 12 gumdrops of one color,
  and 6 each of 2 other colors
• Box of toothpicks

1. Select one color gumdrop for
each of the following elements:

carbon C

hydrogen H

oxygen O

2. Using toothpicks and the correct gumdrops, make a model of:

fruit sugar
$C_6H_{12}O_6$

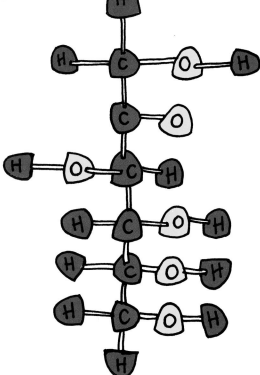

My kitchen contains many things
that can be used in mixing
and chemistry.

A lot of chemistry goes on in the kitchen.
Remember that all of the foods we eat are chemicals.
Cooks are actually **chemists**!

1. Select a substance from the list. Predict what will happen when it is combined with water. Do you think it will dissolve? (That is, after stirring, you won't see it anymore.)

2. Fill a glass half full with water and then add a spoonful of the substance.
Stir with the spoon and see what happens.

Was your prediction right?

3. Repeat the first two steps for each substance on the list.

4. You can also combine three or four substances at the same time. Predict what will happen before you combine them.

Is chemistry just mixing things together or is it making completely new and different things?

Mixing is only one small part of chemistry, but it is an important beginning. A chemist needs to study what happens when things are mixed. Sometimes mixed substances make new chemicals and sometimes they don't. Occassionally you have to wait a while before you can be sure what has happened. Let's do an experiment to see what I mean.

1. Fill the bottle half full with water. Add 8 drops of food coloring

2. Screw the cap on and shake the bottle.

What has happened?

3. Open the bottle and add enough vegetable oil to fill half of the remaining space in the bottle.

4. Put on the cap and again shake the bottle vigorously. What has happened this time?

Does it change while you watch?

Some liquids cannot be mixed. No matter how much you shake them, they will separate from one another when they are left alone!

Is baking bread chemistry?

All cooking is chemistry, including baking bread.
The chemicals are the ingredients you start out with.
If you mix them correctly, you can wind up with something
completely new — a loaf of bread!

1. In one bowl, combine 1 cup of flour, the yeast, and the salt.

You will need
- Help from an adult
- 2 large bowls
- A little more than 3 cups of flour
- 1 teaspoon of salt
- 1 package of active dry yeast (from the grocery store)
- 1 cup of warm water
- 1 tablespoon of oil
- Clean dishtowel
- Tablespoon
- Oven (preheated to 375 degrees)
- 8" x 4" x 2" greased loaf pan
- Wire rack
- Kitchen timer or clock

2. Add the warm water and mix very well with the spoon.

3. Add two more cups of flour. Mix and knead the contents of the bowl (the dough) with your hands.

4. Put the dough onto a lightly floured, smooth clean surface.

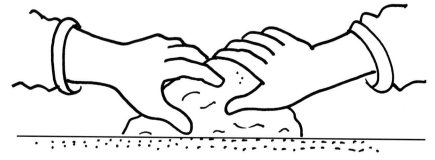

Knead with your hands until the dough is smooth and elastic. This takes about 8-10 minutes.

Continued on the next page.

5. Shape the dough into a ball.

6. With the oil, lightly grease the inside of the second bowl. Place the ball of dough in it.

Turn the ball of dough over once to grease its entire surface.

7. Cover the bowl with a clean dishtowel.

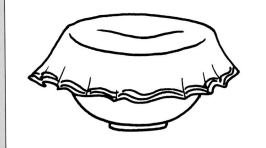

8. Place the bowl in a warm place until the dough rises. It will double in size.

This takes about 1½ to 2 hours to happen.

9. After the dough rises, take it out of the bowl and put it on a lightly floured, clean surface. Punch it several times with your fist to get out any air that formed in the dough while it was rising.

Continued on the next page.

10. Cover the dough with the clean dishtowel. Let the dough rest for 10 minutes.

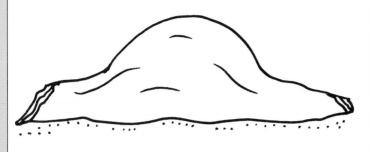

11. Shape the dough into a loaf and place it into the greased loaf pan.

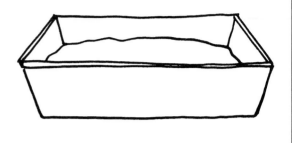

12. Cover the pan with the clean dishtowel and let it rise again until it almost doubles in size (about 45 minutes).

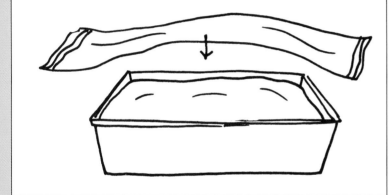

13. Bake the dough in a preheated oven (set at 375 degrees) for about 40 to 45 minutes.

14. When finished baking, have an adult remove the pan from the oven. Take the bread out of the pan and let it cool on a wire rack.

Enjoy your fresh baked bread!
Try spreading some butter and jelly on it.

Can making candy be chemistry?

20

Making any type of food, even candy, is chemistry.
Let's do some more kitchen chemistry and make chocolate!

You will need
- Help from an adult
- Water
- Double boiler
- 2 ounces cocoa
- 4 ounces cocoa butter
- 4 ounces confectioner's sugar
- Spoon
- Stovetop
- 1 ounce chocolate chips
- Tray (or other container) to mold the candy
- Kitchen timer or clock

1. Place water in the bottom part of the double boiler.

2. Mix all of the ingredients except the chips in the top part of the double boiler.

3. Put the double boiler together. Have an adult place it on the stovetop over a medium heat. Stir continuously until everything has melted.

4. Add the chips and stir to mix them in.

5. Use the spoon to pour the chocolate syrup onto the tray in small cookie-sized circles. Let the candy cool for 30 minutes to harden. Then enjoy eating your chemical creation!

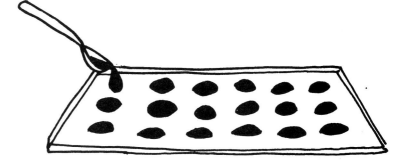

So even making ice cream is chemistry?

Making ice cream is chemistry, and it sure is fun!

You will need
- 1 one-gallon airtight plastic bag
- 1 cup of heavy cream
- 1 tablespoon of sugar
- 1/2 teaspoon of vanilla extract
- 1 two-gallon airtight bag or a large plastic container with a lid
- 48 ice cubes (about 4 ice-cube trays full) or about three pounds of ice
- 1/2 cup of salt
- Mittens
- Kitchen timer or clock

1. Using the one-gallon airtight plastic bag, combine the heavy cream, the sugar, and the vanilla.

2. Seal the bag carefully.

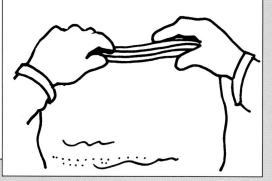

3. Put the ice cubes in the larger bag or plastic container and pour the salt on the ice.

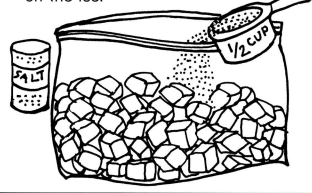

4. Put the smaller bag with the cream mixture into the bag with the ice and seal the larger bag. Put on your mittens and shake the bags for 15 minutes.

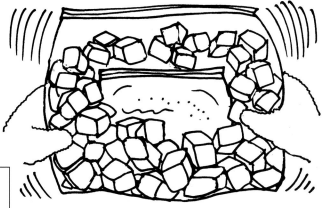

5. Remove the one-gallon bag and taste your ice cream.

You can make flavored ice cream by adding some fruit, such as strawberries, or chocolate.

Where does the fizz in a bottle of soda come from?

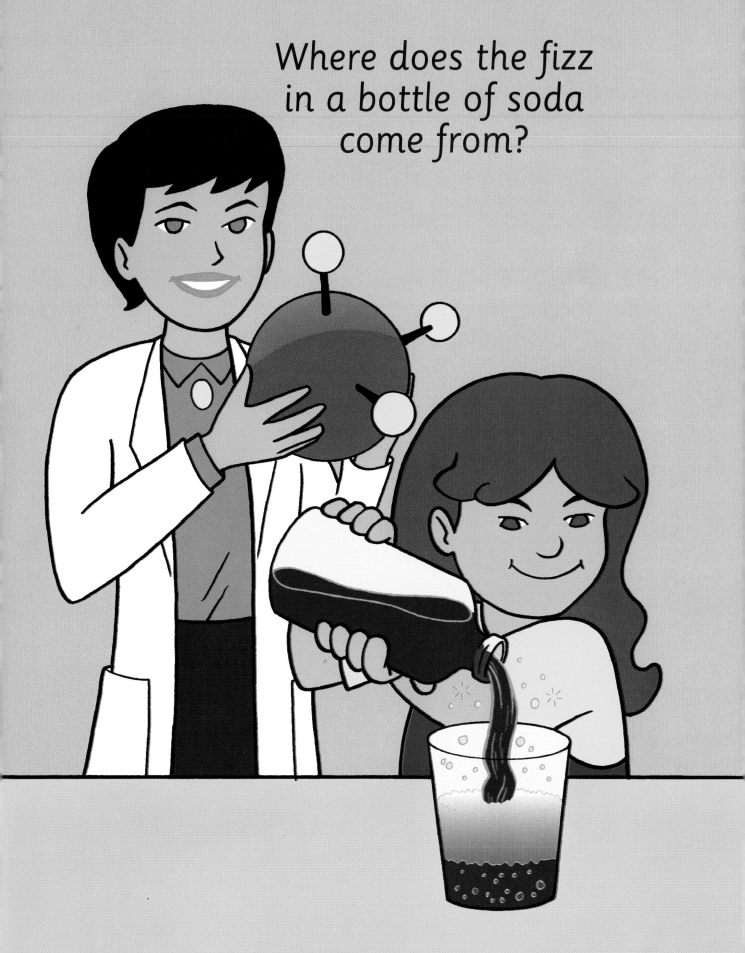

The fizz in soda is carbon dioxide gas. You made a model of this molecule in an earlier activity *(page 9)*. You can make this gas yourself and also see how chemistry changes the taste of something!

1. Fill a cup half full with orange juice and take a taste.

You will need
- Plastic cup
- Orange juice
- ¼ Teaspoon
- Baking soda

2. Add ¼ teaspoon of baking soda to the cup and stir.

3. When a layer of bubbles covers the top of the orange juice, take a sip to see how the taste has changed.

You created carbon dioxide gas and made an orange soda. Did you like the taste?

Do the bubbles in soda last forever?

Let's do an experiment to find out whether the fizz in soda disappears.

1. Label the glasses and bottles 1, 2, and 3. Open bottle 1 and let it sit on the kitchen counter for one day.

You will need
- 3 unopened bottles of soda
- 3 clear plastic glasses
- Marker

2. One day later, pour soda from bottle 1 into glass 1. Open bottle 2 and pour soda into glass 2.

3. Take bottle 3 outside. Shake up the bottle and be careful opening it. Take it back inside and pour soda into glass 3.

4. Compare the different glasses of soda.

How can I catch the gas that is in soda?

Let's make carbon dioxide gas again, but this time you'll make it a different way so you can capture it.

1. Fill the bottle half full with vinegar.

2. Place a teaspoon of baking soda inside the balloon.

3. Keeping the baking soda in the balloon, stretch the open end of the balloon over the mouth of the bottle.

4. Firmly hold the attached end of the balloon in place with your fist.

5. With your other hand, lift the end of the balloon, letting the baking soda fall into the bottle. What happens?

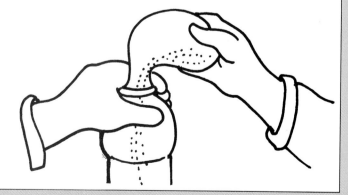

When the baking soda reacts with the vinegar, a gas is produced. Since there was nowhere for the gas to escape, it blew up the balloon!

29

The gas in soda isn't the only type of gas, is it?

30

Carbon dioxide is only one type of gas. It is the gas we exhale (breathe out) and it is the gas that plants need to grow. Helium gas is used in balloons. Neon is used in the orange-colored signs we see at night in store windows. Natural gas is used in stoves. We breathe oxygen gas, which we need to stay alive. Let's do an experiment to produce oxygen gas.

1. Pour a small amount of hydrogen peroxide into the cup.

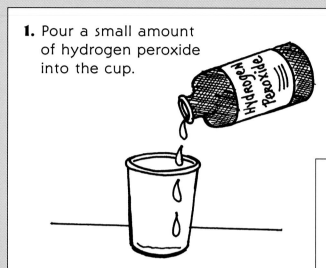

You will need
- Plastic cup
- Hydrogen peroxide (from the drugstore)
- Plastic knife
- Potato

2. Use the plastic knife to remove the skin and cut out a small piece of raw potato.

3. Place the piece of potato in the hydrogen peroxide.

4. The small bubbles that form around the potato are oxygen bubbles.

Does chemistry include separating or taking things apart?

Chemistry includes separating materials.
If you mix pepper and water, you could try to take each
piece of pepper out one at a time, but that would be hard.
Let's learn an easier way to separate pepper from water.

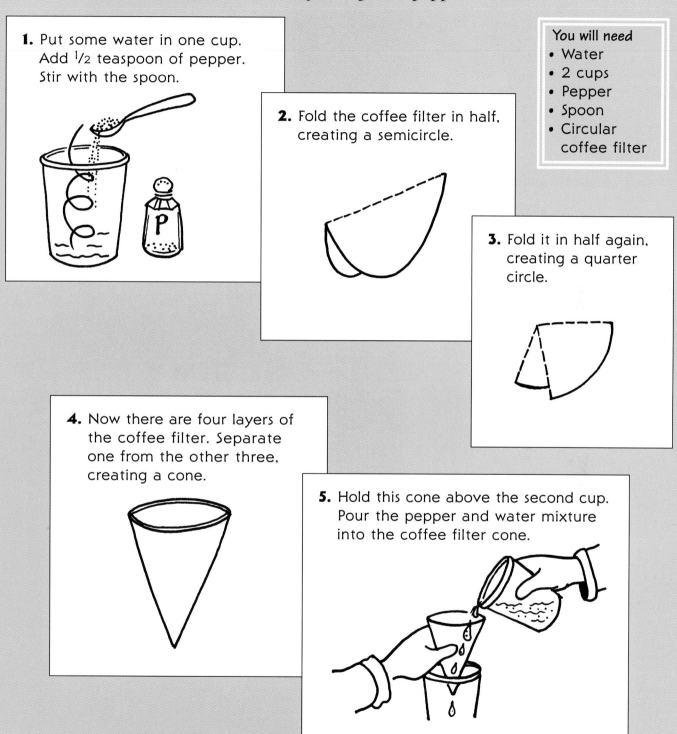

1. Put some water in one cup. Add ¹/₂ teaspoon of pepper. Stir with the spoon.

You will need
• Water
• 2 cups
• Pepper
• Spoon
• Circular coffee filter

2. Fold the coffee filter in half, creating a semicircle.

3. Fold it in half again, creating a quarter circle.

4. Now there are four layers of the coffee filter. Separate one from the other three, creating a cone.

5. Hold this cone above the second cup. Pour the pepper and water mixture into the coffee filter cone.

The coffee filter has small openings. Only things smaller than these openings will get through. What passes through is called the **filtrate**. What stays in the filter paper is called the **residue**. In this case, water is the filtrate and pepper is the residue. You can try to use this method to separate other mixtures!

What about something like milk?
Can that be separated into different parts?

Do you remember the story of how Little Miss Muffett was eating her curds and whey? Curds and whey are different parts of milk. Curds are the part used to make cheese. However, you will have to do some chemistry before you can separate the curds from the whey.

1. Fill one cup a third of the way with milk.

2. Add enough vinegar to fill the cup to the halfway point.

You will need
- 2 cups
- 1/2 cup of milk
- Vinegar
- Spoon
- Circular coffee filter

3. Stir with the spoon. You now have curds and whey.

4. Fold the coffee filter to make a cone as shown in steps 2-4 of the previous experiment (on page 33).

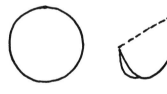

5. Place the filter cone over the second cup and slowly pour the curds and whey into the cone.

The residue is the curds and the filtrate is the whey.

35

What is inside a marker must be chemicals. Can they be separated?

The chemicals that are in the marker are called **pigments**.
You can separate them by using a different process.

> **You will *need***
> • Circular coffee filters
> • Various water-soluble markers
> • Water
> • Spoon

1. Spread out a coffee filter and draw a circle with one marker.

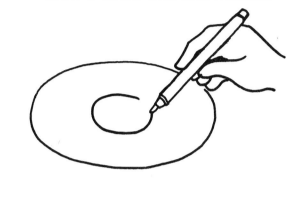

2. Place one or two spoonfuls of water in the middle of the circle.

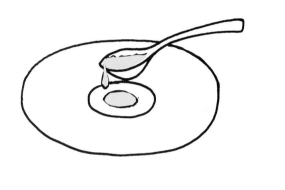

3. Watch what happens!

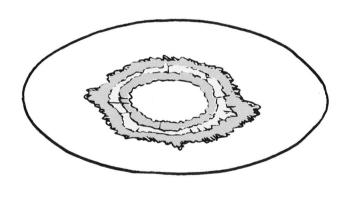

4. Use separate coffee filters to test each marker.

If the marker contains more than one pigment, they will move apart at different speeds. They want to go with the spreading water while they also want to stay attached to the paper. Some pigments will be more strongly attracted by the water molecules while others are more strongly attracted to the paper. This process is called **chromatography** and what you made are called **chromatograms**!

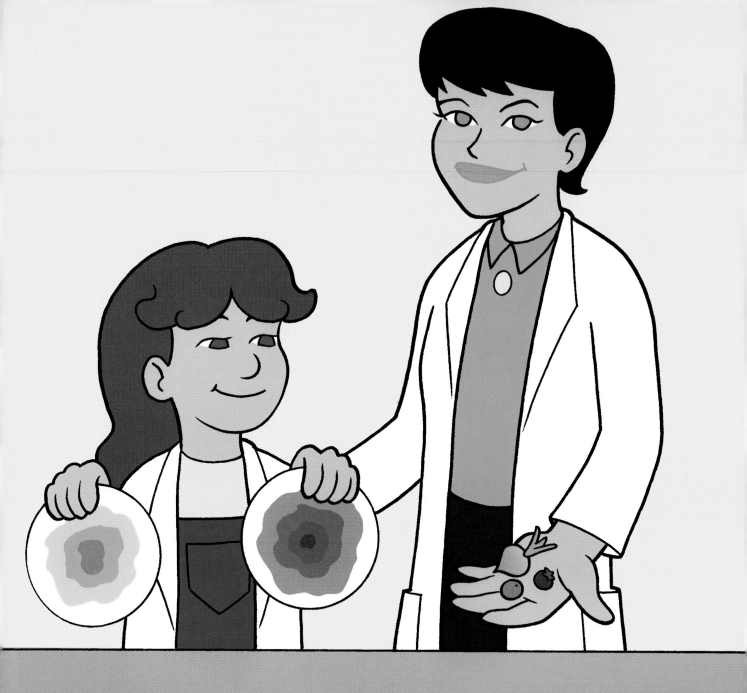

Chemistry can separate colors.
Can it change one color into
another color?

Many items contain dyes that give each item its particular color. Some dyes change color when other chemicals combine with them. These dyes are called **indicators**. Let's test some common dyes to see if they are indicators.

1. Place a heaping teaspoon of baking soda in one glass. Fill the glass two-thirds of the way with water. Stir with the spoon to make a solution.

You will need
- Baking soda
- Large, clear drinking glass
- Hot water
- 9 white paper cups
- Vinegar
- 5 teaspoons
- Beet juice
- Cranberry juice
- Blueberry juice

2. Fill three paper cups halfway with water. Add a teaspoon of beet juice to each.

3. Add a teaspoon of vinegar to one cup of the beet juice.

Add a teaspoon of the baking soda solution to the second cup of beet juice.

Compare the three solutions of beet juice.

Vinegar Solution

Baking Soda Solution

Plain Beet Juice

Beet Juice + Vinegar

Beet Juice + Baking-Soda Solution

4. Repeat this with cranberry juice and blueberry juice.

Vinegar is **acidic**. Baking soda is **basic**. Dyes that change color when these chemicals are added are called **acid-base indicators**. If it is summer, you can also collect different flowers, crush them in some warm water, and test to see if they are acid-base indicators by seeing whether the color changes with the addition of vinegar or baking-soda solution.

I heard that acid rain is bad.
Are all acids bad?

There are many acids. We use acids to do a lot of things. We have to be careful with some dangerous acids, but there are many common acids all around us. Vitamin C is an acid. So are aspirin and vinegar. Let's do an experiment to see why people are concerned about acid rain.

You will need
- 2 clear cups
- Vinegar
- Piece of chalk
- Piece of a seashell

1. Place some vinegar in each cup.

2. Place the piece of chalk in one cup.

3. Place the piece of seashell in the other cup.

4. Watch what happens.

All acids can eat away at certain materials, such as limestone and many metals. Chalk and seashells are made of limestone. If there is too much acid in the rain, it can harm cars, buildings, and statues.

What makes
a stamp stick
to an envelope?

Substances can stick to themselves or to other substances, depending on conditions and the properties of the chemicals. When you lick a stamp, the chemical conditions change. As it dries, a stamp becomes attached to an envelope. Let's do an experiment to better understand this.

You will need
- Help from an adult
- Pot of boiling water
- Box of spaghetti
- Strainer
- Bowl

1. Have an adult bring a pot of water to a boil. Add the spaghetti to the pot. Watch how the hot water changes the spaghetti.

2. When the spaghetti is cooked, use the strainer to separate the spaghetti from the water.

3. Place some of the spaghetti in a bowl. Let it sit until it cools down and it dries out — the water evaporates (goes away). Investigate how the spaghetti has changed.

When the spaghetti was cooking, it was similar to the molecules on a stamp after it has been licked. In each case, the water is making the molecules able to bend and move. As the water evaporated from the stamp and the spaghetti, the molecules attached to whatever they were touching, which included each other and, in the case of the stamp, the envelope or, in the case of the spaghetti, the bowl.

How do different tapes work?

You can compare how well different types of tape stick to themselves and to other surfaces. Some of the results may surprise you!

You will need
- A variety of tapes: cellophane, masking, packing, electrical, post-it, duct tape
- Various surfaces: wooden table, window, refrigerator door

1. Take two pieces of one type of tape and attach them together, sticky side to sticky side.

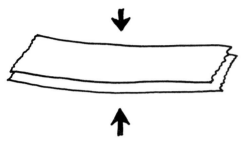

2. See how easy it is to separate them by peeling them apart at the same end.

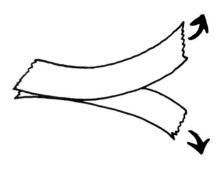

3. Try this again, but now try to pull them apart from opposite ends, keeping them facing one another.

Repeat this test for each type of tape.

4. Take a piece of one tape and attach it to a surface. See how easy it is to remove the tape, both by peeling and by pulling.
Repeat this step
with each of the other tapes.
Try this on the various surfaces.

Glues and pastes
are also chemicals, right?

You can do the chemistry needed to make your own glue.
You can then test to see how well it works.

You will need
- 5 ounces of skim milk in a cup
- 1 ounce of vinegar
- 2 teaspoons
- 8" x 8" square of cotton cloth
- Water
- 1 cup
- Baking soda
- Pieces of paper (to test the glue)

1. Add 1 ounce of vinegar to the 5 ounces of skim milk.

1 ounce vinegar

5 ounces skim milk

2. Stir with the spoon. The curds will separate from the whey.

3. Set the cloth square over the second cup, making a pocket in the cup.

4. Slowly pour all of the contents of the first cup into the cloth.

Continued on the next page.

5. Twist the ends of the cloth together and then squeeze out the rest of the whey. This can be poured down the drain.

6. Use the spoon to scrape the curds back into the first cup.

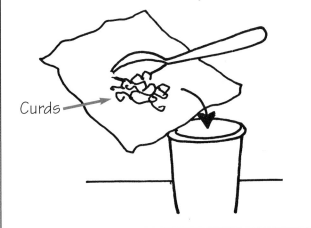

Curds

7. Add 2 teaspoons of water into the cup. Use the spoon to break up the curds and then stir the mixture.

Continued on the next page.

48

8. With the second spoon add about ¹/₂ teaspoon of baking soda to the cup. Watch for bubbling and add just a little more baking soda until no more bubbles appear.

Now you have made glue!

9. Test how well the glue works.
Apply some to one piece of paper.

10. Now stick that piece of paper with the glue on it to a second plain piece of paper. Once the glue dries, try pulling the pieces of paper apart.
What happens?

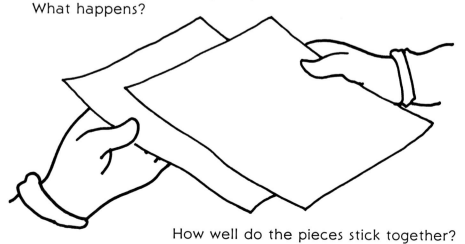

How well do the pieces stick together?

Can chemists make fun stuff that does more interesting things?

There are chemicals that do what you expect and then there are others that can surprise you. Let's try to make one that acts differently when you change the force that you apply.

1. Fill the container halfway with cornstarch.

You will *need*
- 16 oz. deli container
- Cornstarch
- Water
- Spoon

2. Add water, a little at a time, stirring with the spoon.

3. Stop stirring when cracks form behind the spoon and then seem to melt together.

4. Try pushing your finger in slowly.

What happens?

5. Try pushing your finger in very quickly!

What happens?

The water molecules and cornstarch move aside when your finger is pushed in slowly. However, when you try to push it in quickly, the molecules are still attracted to one another and they stop your finger!

51

A putty sticks to itself
and sometimes to other things.
Is it easy to make a putty?

There are many different types of putties. They are often used to fill cracks, but some are interesting to play with, experimenting to see how they respond to different **forces**.

1. Place a small quantity of white glue in the bowl.

You will **need**
- Soup bowl
- Spoon
- White liquid glue
- Liquid starch
  (from a grocery store)

2. Add half as much liquid starch to the white glue.

3. Mix the materials together with the spoon.

4. Lift the putty in your hands and experiment to see what happens when you squeeze it, pull it apart slowly, and pull it apart quickly.

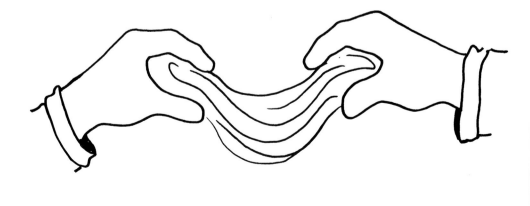

Can we make a chemical that bounces?

Some putties can bounce. Let's see how to make one.

1. Fill one cup halfway with water and add a spoonful of borax. Stir. Some of the borax should still be visible at the bottom after you stir.

1.

You will *need*
- 3 clear cups (5-ounce plastic cups work well)
- Water
- Borax (from the detergent aisle at the supermarket)
- White liquid glue
- Food coloring
- 2 spoons

2. Add enough white glue to the second cup to fill it a quarter of the way.

1.   2.

3. Add an equal quantity of water so the cup is half full.

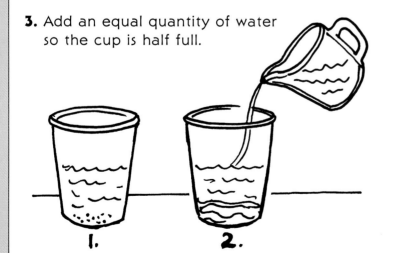

1.   2.

4. Then add a drop or two of food coloring.

2.

Continued on the next page.

55

5. Stir this together with the second spoon.

6. Pour half of the colored glue and water mixture into the third cup.

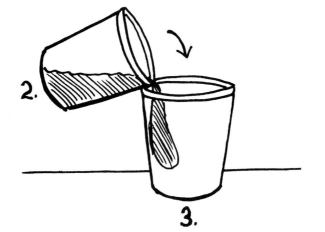

7. Add an equal amount of the borax and water mixture to the third cup.

Continued on the next page.

8. Stir this combination together.
It will change to something very different.

3.

9. Take out the putty, squeeze out the liquid,
and roll it into a ball in your hands.

10. Test to see if your ball will bounce
when you drop it on a hard surface.

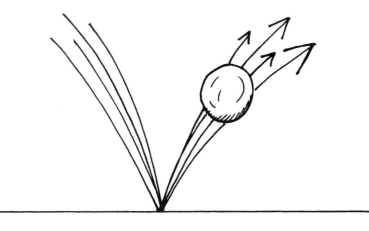

Glossary

acid — a chemical which releases hydrogen ions in water and has a sour taste

acid-base indicators — chemicals which turn one color in the presence of an acid and a different color in the presence of a base

acid rain — rain that contains more than the natural amount of acid, due to pollution released from cars, factories, etc.

acidic — having the properties of an acid

atoms — the simplest building block of chemicals

base — a chemical which reacts with an acid to produce water molecules

basic — having the properties of a base

chemical — any substance which has mass and takes up space, whether a solid, liquid, or gas

chemist — a scientist who specializes in chemistry

chemistry — the study of chemicals and how they react

chromatogram — a picture in which chemicals have been separated by color

chromatography — separating chemicals based on color

crystal — a solid substance in which the molecules are arranged in a repeating pattern

force — energy that causes or changes motion

filtrate — the material which passes through a filter

indicator — a chemical which changes color in the presence of certain other chemicals

molecule — the simplest unit of a chemical, made of one or more atoms

pigment — a chemical used to give color to paint

putty — a soft mixture of chemicals which can be shaped to fill a mold or crack

residue — the material which is trapped by a filter

saturated solution — is when the liquid is completely full of a solid